A little Bit of Peace and Me

Kelsey Reblin

By Kelsey Reblin

The events are true, but the names have been changed for privacy reasons.
copyright © 2019 by Kelsey Reblin

Library of Congress Control Number:
2020900163

ISBN: 978-1-64713-642-0
Printed in the United States of America

Book Cover designed by J. Duclos
Illustrations: Cat arch angel/adobe.stock

Sheiskelseyreblin
sheiskelseyreblin@gmail.com
www.sheiskelseyreblin.com

Introduction

This book is filled with my journal entries and memoirs that I have written to help motivate myself in times when I've needed uplifting or have documented a new learning experience.

I have found I can truly express myself better as a writer and hope this book serves as many people as possible in a positive manner.

It has been a life long goal of mine to continuously help others.

*... a little bit of self-reflection, gratitude,
and positivity daily can give a lot of peace.*

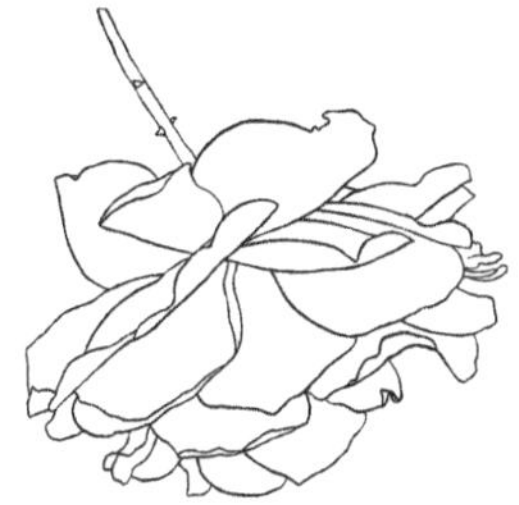

SCARS

Our scars make us beautiful. Our scars may not be visible, but everyone has them. These scars, these moments in life, these experiences are what truly make us as people. Where there is light, there has been darkness. Everyone has felt at times like they have been defeated, or have lost a sense of hope. What matters today is having the strength to get up when you have been knocked down. My experiences have made me who I am and I choose to embrace each and every one of them, for they have sculpted my heart and soul. No matter how big or small any given struggle may be, it matters because it makes us who we are. We are constantly healing. We are constantly growing. Life will get in the way at some point or another, but you can't let that stop you from reaching your goals. Remember that you can be your own hero and I suggest that you surround yourself with those who support you. I would not be where I am today if it wasn't for the compassion, the love, the strength, the empathy, and kindness of others. We must believe the universe works for, and not against, us. Keep your faith and wear your scars with pride.

Surround yourself with those who support you
and will allow you to grow in a healthy way.

MEDICINE

Music is medicine.
The outdoors is medicine.
Laughter is medicine.
We as people are medicine.
Discover your own medicine.
Don't forget that sometimes the simplest things in life can
have an enormous positive impact for our health.

Facing challenges in life can be scary. Fear often creeps up on you right before the start of a new journey. The truth is that if we never challenge ourselves in life, then we don't give ourselves the chance and opportunity to grow.

HARD WORK

Do not work to prove something to others. Work hard in life
for yourself. Don't forget all the positive accomplishments
from your past. We are naturally the hardest on ourselves.
Even small accomplishments are big wins. By taking
care of ourselves we naturally take care of others.

I am a fighter. I will not give up. I have goals and ambition. I am determined. I am independent. I have fire within me. I am powerful.

WEEKLY PLANNING

Sunday is the day before most of us will head back to work after the weekend. Something that has served me well is creating positive rituals, good habits, and staying consistent. On Sunday, I like to write a list of what I need to do to get ready for the week. Meal prepping, exercising, and getting adequate rest is a great way to prepare. Practicing these habits allows us to focus, be attentive and uphold our short- and long-term goals. Being consistent and dedicated is a necessary daily/ weekly practice. You do not get good at anything permanently by just "winging" it, or by relying on continuous good "luck." The best of the best, the people who prepare for the week on Sunday, these are the ones who will continuously attract and obtain success.

Never forget that it is the little things that can make a difference in your life or someone else's. For example, a simple smile could change someone's entire day.

BATTLES

Time and time again, we watch ourselves fall into the same trap. A trap of recurring vicious cycles that suppress our greater good. We must learn, act, and grow from our mistakes. If we continue to play that record of our past mistakes, that same sad song will continue to play in our lives. Awareness is the first step to change. Knowing something isn't right or is holding you back from being the best version of yourself is the first key to success. You have the power to make your own choices for the benefit of your life. Every single day we can do small acts to improve ourselves. Remember to stop fighting the battles you've already won. Move forward and fight for bigger and better things in life. Have great expectations to allow yourself to be the best human being you can possibly be. Ask yourself today, *Do I keep fighting the same battles in my life? Why is this happening? How can I control this issue?* The first step is to put a stop to the cycle.

Empower others by revealing their strengths.

REST AND RECOVERY

Let us give our body and mind the daily restoration they need.
If you want to think clearly, feel good, and feel energized, you
have to give both your body and mind the chance to recover.

Human connection is not always built around what
brings us together in commonalities, but rather
by the appreciation and the bonds we share when
embracing our individualities and differences.

COMMITMENT

Last Saturday I had brunch with my boyfriend at a bagel shop.
I think it's perfectly healthy and beautiful for any couple
to sit down and discuss what may be important both for
today and in the future. Having a partner is not about being
perfect for him or her, but to appreciate that as a team you
can use your strengths to assist each other's weaknesses.
One of us may be lacking or in need of guidance. For example,
I may know more about health, and my boyfriend might know
more about finances, so we rely on each other's strengths to
cover our weaknesses in those areas. Use the tools in your
pockets to amplify the relationship.

Our perception determines our reality. Thinking
a task is difficult will cause it to be difficult.

DON'T GIVE UP

Never let anyone or anything make you close your mind to your own abilities. Any negativity that comes across your path, shake it off and let it go, because it will not serve you. When someone shares that they don't believe in your dreams, that's their own limiting belief; one they have about themselves. If you were to become fulfilled, it might make them feel uneasy. When it comes to your dreams and goals, drop any thoughts that something cannot be done. It's also important to remember: Good things take time. If your approach to your goal doesn't work the first time, change the plan. Take what you've learned and use that to excel on the second or third attempt. Don't give up because it didn't work out on the first try! Trust yourself, trust in your heart, trust in the drive that forces you to persist in the direction you'd like to go.

In this life we must not only survive, but THRIVE.

REFLECTION IN SAN DIEGO

Last night my boyfriend planned to take his best friends and me
to this exquisite restaurant on the water with this incredible view
of downtown San Diego. There were three beautiful practices I
took away from this happy hour with close friends. (1.) Try new
things even if it scares you sometimes. I am not a huge fan of
shellfish, but the mussels I tried were great! (2.) Take care of those
that take care of you. You don't have to make huge gestures in
this. A small card, for example, can be a big deal. (3.) Enjoy the
view no matter where you are. Life is precious and its beauty
shouldn't be ignored. Take it in, take a picture, store it in your memory.

We must practice and incorporate healthy actions into our lives
so that new pathways and opportunities can be introduced.

YOGA MAT

This morning I attended hot yoga. I took my yoga mat out of my closet and it was hard and bent in areas. To be honest, I was worried it wasn't going to flatten out when I got to class. I made it to yoga though, and as soon as we started, I felt like my body was just like my hard and bent mat. Not a good feeling! At first, I was upset with myself . Then I realized that showing up today was a good way to tell my body "Sorry" and awaken my mind. Giving myself this hour on my crinkled mat, I set the intention to give myself self-love.

Working through my emotions that came up on my mat today, I remembered a few things. What is self-love? To me, self-love is creating a life for yourself that you are so undeniably in love with that you don't worry about other's perceptions. When it comes to mind-body health, we must be honest with ourselves, but also not be so hard. Maybe we wouldn't be so hard if we just did what we know our body needs. Good diet, exercise, time to settle the mind and regain/establish/sharpen our mental clarity.

Remember, self-love and self-confidence are not the same thing. We must have self-confidence to believe in the actions we take in life. We must have self-love to ensure the outside/social demands from society don't corrupt our inner peace. When we take actions to prove ourselves to others, or feel accepted, that is not coming from a place of self-love. Practice and commit to loving yourself wholeheartedly by giving what you know your body and mind needs to feel good. That is why you need self-confidence, to be able to take action on what makes you feel good in life.

By the end of the practice, I looked down at my mat. It was now completely flattened. I know it will take more than one time to establish my goals of good health with this practice, but today I proved to myself—and I hope it will prove to others—how one hour of committing to your mind and body can really make a positive impact on your life.

Change and transformation takes commitment and dedication.

BLOSSOMING BEAUTY

25

Looking as if it is still in its early stages of blossoming, yet this flower already has a vast amount of beauty to share with the world. I feel that we all forget how beautiful we are during the process of growth. We must remember that growth takes time. Not minutes, days, or even months. It can take years. We must be patient, and let the beauty that we withhold shine.

The people in your life, the food you take in, the sun on your face, are just a few of the many things that play a major role in your health and success.

EXPRESSIONS OF LOVE

Everyone has some way or form in which they share their love.
Sometimes I like to write song lyrics for my boyfriend; he refers
to it as poetry. Sometimes it's hard to have our love and affection
received the exact way we want. We think to ourselves, *Please feel
what I feel.* The truth is, we all express ourselves differently. A part
of love is appreciating of the many ways love is given to us. To have
gratitude. Let us spread love and light in our own way and also be
open to receiving the unique love and light that is given to us.

As I've gotten older, I am reminded to be mindful and reach
out to my best friends and family from time to time.
It is likely, we are all guilty of not doing these things enough.

STRENGTHS

When struggling with something in life, it's important to remember your strengths, and not beat yourself up over your weaknesses. I've practiced this with others—and need to practice this more with myself. We all have weaknesses, but we also all have strengths. If we continuously stress upon the weaknesses more than our strengths, it will be a constant battle between fear and faith. Try to stress what is going right in your life and how that can progress, instead of what is going wrong.

You only have one body, fuel it with good food, positive
thoughts, and exercise it as much as possible. Every
car needs an oil change, so does your body.

LOSS

Healing from the loss of someone special takes time. Healing
is slow. It can take months and years. In my own life, the
one thing I know in looking back at photos is that they
give me happy thoughts about our memories; calm,
loving, and joyful thoughts. Although your loss is a deep
burning pain to my soul, your light will still shine on the rest
of the world, and will forever be inside my heart.

Embrace the biggest forms of love, compassion, care,
and joy by our brilliant human connections.

SHOW UP

It's pretty simple. If you care about something, or someone, and your own success, you will show up in some way or form. The less you show up, the more things will fade. We have to create what we want for ourselves. If there is one thing you can continue to do for yourself today, it is, quite simply, to just show up.

The only person you need to believe that you
can accomplish something, is you.

PATIENCE

Let your energy be used to build, not destroy. Sometimes it may take a lot more patience to build—rather than destroy—with your energy. At times we must become aware of the energy we give off to the world, and also of the energy we are receiving. You are much more likely to impact someone else's life by allowing yourself to share your positivity (vs. negativity). By having a positive reaction to a negative situation or comment, it allows for the flow of energy that has built up to remain. Be consistent. Catch yourself when you feel you are becoming cold, annoyed, or impatient with others. Are you really upset with them? We must look within ourselves to understand what energy we are giving out to the world. Why am I becoming so reactive to this person or situation? How can I respond better to positively influence my own life and others? These are questions that mindfulness practice and self-awareness will naturally cause to arise in one's mind in times of controversy. Give love, share positivity, be lighthearted, and hold on to the power of calm, especially when it can be so easy to switch to a mood that can destroy others, or your own, energy. Share your light. Don't dim others thinking your light will shine brighter.

Invest your time with those who've invested in you—and for the right reasons. Not for money, fame, or small entertainment, but simply because they enjoy you as a person.

FIGHT OR FLIGHT

Calmness is a superpower. Our minds and bodies are constantly in fight or flight mode. We must pause and give our body and mind time for rest and peace through meditation, yoga, and exercise—or whatever action/practice that may settle you completely in heart, mind, and body. Give back to your body and mind what it has given to you.

To motivate and inspire, we must paint a full picture
of our greatest accomplishments to others.

A FRIENDLY REMINDER

Let's focus less on our problems and more on our purpose. Let your purpose—not your problems—fuel you with motivation and strength.

It is the hardest moments, the moments where you must dig down to never give up, when great things occur.

THINKING BIGGER

If you want bigger and better things in life, you have to become aware
of what might be dragging you down. Treat small tasks like big tasks
and you will most likely be more successful when it comes to taking
on something more challenging. Become aware of your routine,
because without us realizing it, we are people with continuous
repetitive actions and behaviors. Set your goals and reflect, daily,
on those routines to observe what you can do better to make those
goals happen. Growth as a person takes time, it takes will power,
and it takes work. Instead of thinking you have to make huge
changes to make something happen, take a step back and look at
the small things in your daily routine. Understanding and becoming
aware of our habits and behaviors can make life a lot easier.

Express yourself. Don't suppress yourself.

KELSEY'S RECIPE FOR LIFE:

- Love yourself

- Strive for good health

- Be creative

- Find strength from your strengths (you have a lot)

- Never stop learning

- Strive for growth

- Optimism opens doors

- Let go of what you cannot control

- Value yourself and know your worth

- Get to know people for who they are, not because they look
a certain way or have some certain lifestyle you want

- Help others when you can

- Think of others (send a thoughtful text, for example)

- If you appreciate someone or something, express that feeling

- Surround yourself with people who bring positivity to your life

- If you want to be successful, commit yourself 100 percent

- Smile more

- Stay light-hearted

- Have a voice if you wish to be heard

- Be mindful

- Meditate

- Reduce stress

- Enjoy the little things

People will come and go in our lives. Friend groups grow smaller, but become greater in value.

GOALS

It is vital to have short-term goals to be able to obtain your long
- term goals. For example, great athletes don't just wake up one
day ready to compete against the best of the best in the world.
One should be proud of short-term goals but SERIOUSLY, it's
when you nail those long-term goals, after all your hard work
and dedication, that keep lifelong gratification in your heart and
mind. Write down your long-term goals and hold that vision.
Then write down the short-term goals to work on yourself and
use that daily lifestyle to reach the long-term aspirations.

Give true direction and understanding of the depths to where you have been to get where you are. Not to discourage, or give doubt, but just to be real, honest, and truthful.

FOUNDATION FOR GOALS

Today I realized that, with all the work I've done the last few years, I'm only stepping on the brakes and going in reverse to rebuild the foundation that I needed from the start. There is no such thing as "failure" or "starting completely over." The hard work, the passion, and vision is not forgotten when rebuilding structure into your life. I can either aspire for new goals in the future or work off the other things I've put time into already. It's a win-win situation with the tool of self-awareness. The ability to pause and recognize what's been holding you back from your dreams is not a sign of weakness, it's a miracle. The true meaning of WHY you do what you do every day, that is your given path.

Giving genuine feedback and encouragement will help someone obtain a goal in a much more productive way. Also, asking for guidance to increase your chance of being successful is not to be looked down upon. It's smart. Even the best athletes in the world still have coaches and mentors on the sideline...even after winning many championships.

WRITE DOWN YOUR GOALS

Never let go of your vision. We have to trust the process of how we reach our goals. Hold that vision hard. Write your vision down. Never let that vision go. Always stay positive even when you hit roadblocks. These blocks are just small peaks of growth in life. They make us blossom into the beautiful souls that we are. Never underestimate yourself. You got this! Hold the vision, trust the process.

It's said that people who help others are usually happier. I believe it. I also believe that the simplest acts of kindness can go a long way. We don't have to do much to be a positive influence in other people's lives. It's good for us to remember that. Continuous small acts of kindness pull people together rather than apart. That is what we need, and have always needed.

LIGHT AND LOVE

May you always see the light in me, as I see the light
in you. May we be grateful for those who take the
time to love and show affection in our lives.

It is our own unique individual experiences in life that make us an asset to the lives that surround us.

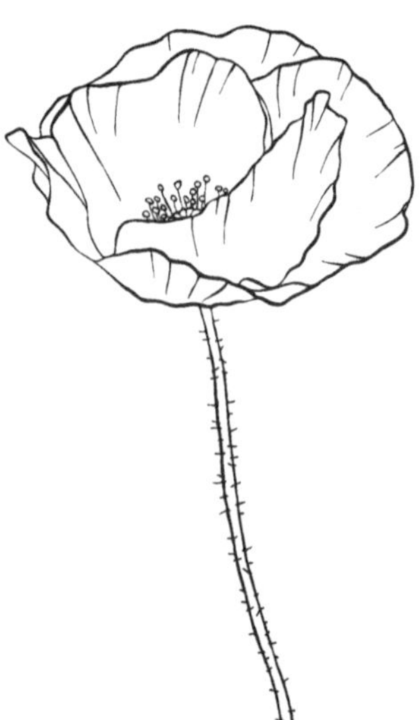

There is always something to learn from others. We will, quite simply, never know it all. Keeping an open mindset is the new "wise" or, rather, the new "intelligent." Learn from others, and grow together.

SELF-LOVE

Some advice I give about relationships is that you must love yourself and love where you are at in life to start or develop a new intimate relationship. Why is this so important? A relationship doesn't mean you should try and fill a void in your life. A relationship is a special connection that allows you to express yourself and amplify your light and love in this world and to this person. It is undeniable that we all want some form of love, whether we admit it or not. We must be brave, vulnerable, and have self-love to open to the opportunity for true love. Relationships are work and compromise. They need skills like being a good listener, as well as patience, honesty, trust, and understanding. Our connections bring us together, but it is our response to our differences and imperfections that reveals true unconditional love.

Being present doesn't only mean being present in the
moment, it means also being present to your own life:
physically, mentally, emotionally, and spiritually.

THE DANCE

We all have motives in life, whether they are thought out consciously—or mysteriously acted out by our subconscious. It is possible that we believe we are making mistakes on our journey, because it is not in a form or way we think it should be or how others should perceive our actions.

Say you are in the middle of dance routine, and you suddenly stumble on a move. You have two options. Ruin the entire dance and start all over again, or improvise with some transitional move that can replace the mistake. What would honestly motivate or inspire you? For me, starting the dance all over again would most likely make me feel bad about myself—and possibly feel like a broken record that can't get a dance routine correct. By choosing to play off of the mistake, we create a positive mindset that allows for a better outlook of ourselves. Those watching the dance might not even notice that you have made a mistake.

Sometimes when I make mistakes, instead of feeling like a complete mess, I think it would be more helpful to allow myself to see how I can somehow generate a positive outcome. Of course, we must be self-aware of why we choose some actions, but be weary of mixing passion, purpose, and drive with punishment. If we can learn how our own heart and mind operates, then we can properly manage our actions to turn our choices into better plans with less mistakes. Today, take a look at yourself from the inside out. Ask yourself, *Why do I act in certain ways? Why do I take certain actions? Am I acting out of pure stupidity or am I hoping to create a reality for myself that is longing in my heart and body?* Remember to learn from your mistakes and see the value in the challenge and process of growth. The song will continue to play, so just keep dancing.

Remember to never be ashamed of your past or present. You are on your own journey. Little may we know that someone else could be going through something similar.

ADAPTATION TO CHANGE

In life, we can experience many changes, but we have to look at them in a positive light. Take your experiences and evaluate what you learned from them and how they helped you grow as a person. Just because you don't stay on the same path, doesn't mean you have failed or are a failure. When we think we have failed, we are often hard on ourselves. Life takes twists and turns, and some turns might be the wrong way, but all that matters is that you utilize your experiences—ultimately—to keep you moving in the directions of your dreams.

Look ahead, look at how far you've come, look within,
look to see all the beauty in the world and in yourself.

ROCK BOTTOM

Whatever you do, don't stop doing what you know is best for you. Don't stop fighting for the life you want. If you want inner peace, get inner peace. If you want success, fight and work hard for your success. Remember, it shouldn't take the taste of pavement to your face to get yourself back up, to keep moving forward, to find motivation, to find energy. No matter what happens, keep fighting and being persistent in the direction of your dreams. Sometimes it takes a quick reminder of where we have been before and where we are now. No one will ever know what it feels like to be in your shoes. They don't understand the miles you've run—and don't expect them to. The only thing that matters is that they see the light, heart, and fire in your beautiful soul.

Surround yourself with others that make you feel like a somebody. Surround yourself with supportive and loving people. Surround yourself with people who listen.

DATING TODAY

To anyone that is single out there today and feels they will never find someone, just remember to be yourself, love yourself, and trust the process and the universe, that you can find a partner that will love you endlessly. Also, if you feel like a perception of yours hasn't changed in a while about relationships, and you are still not achieving what you want. Change it. Take a step back. *What am I really looking for?* But always remember that you must be your own person and have self-love first. When someone recognizes your light, and appreciates it, that will serve you much more than trying to prove to a partner you're something you are not. Love is a beautiful thing because it's not perfect. A good partner will help you grow. A good partner will allow for a healthy and positive environment.

The sky above allows me to see the light radiating down on my skin. Earth below me gives me sturdiness and a sense of grounding. A fire within me reminds me to never give up, stay motivated, stay positive, and stay excited.

FREE WRITING, TO FREE MY MIND

She takes her mask off and placed it in his hands. This is me.
This is who I am. Do you know what I am thinking? Come find
out what is in my head. Peel back the layers of my soul like an
onion. The depths of a human. The idyllic mind, yet sometimes
mass chaos. The beauty of one heart. Place her in a white room.
Let her paint the walls with color. Let her dance around, free.
Play the music. Play it loud. Hear my mind. Inside out. Love
her inside and out. Her hand placed on your cheek. Her eyes
meet yours. You begin to rise off the ground. You are lost in
her ocean eyes. Drowning. Is this real life? What is love? The
creator of all, you, in this moment. We share the frequency of
this love together. We have the light. We are the light. We are
love. Step by step we keep moving forward, we dance to the beat
of our hearts. Never in shame. You are you. You are alive. To be
alive, what a delightful gift to embrace each and every minute.
Our memories are our treasure chest to the development of
new chapters, new growth. A ray of sunshine touches your sweet
face. For energy may never be lost. It is the energy we share,
dead or alive. We must share and we must always remember.

One person may be a teacher, lover, and friend, all at the same time.

LISTEN

The ability to listen to others is a superpower. Give others the opportunity to speak, for sometimes all one may need is someone to just simply listen.

Sometimes life throws us curveballs, but we have to keep
swinging, no matter what, and adjust to the change. May
we live with gratitude and be present in this beautiful
life we have been given, each and every day.

FULL CUP

She had a cup so full that even when they thought she
hit a wall, she was just making a bigger splash.

Let us discover our own inner beauty.

Sheiskelseyreblin
sheiskelseyreblin@gmail.com
www.sheiskelseyreblin.com

www.ingramcontent.com/pod-product-compliance
Lightning Source LLC
Chambersburg PA
CBHW041223050726
47599CB00001B/54